For my sons, Jason and Lucas

WHAT I WANT TO BE

我的志願

Peter Wilds 著

蔡兆倫 繪

王盟雄 譯

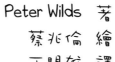

Ladies and gentlemen, boys and girls,

please listen carefully.

The topic of my speech today

is what I want to be.

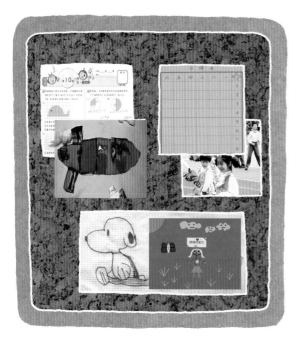

When I grow up I want to teach in many different schools.

I want to be the principal, so *I* can write the rules.

Next I'll be a circus *clown
and walk on shaky *wires,

*為生字，請參照生字表

6

or I might be a firefighter

so I can put out fires.

8

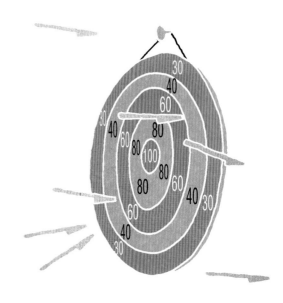

I want to be a heart doctor

so I can save some lives.

(I also look so good in white,

and I can play with knives!)

I'd like to be a movie star

and drive in *limousines,

or I could be a fashion queen

in high-class magazines.

Then I'll be an *astronaut
and fly among the stars.
I'll build a city on the moon
and live on planet *Mars.

My math is good so I can be

a *teller in a bank.

I will join the army next,

so I can drive a tank.

Then I'll be a great painter,

and wear a silly hat,

or be a *sumo wrestler

and let myself get fat.

Next I'll be an *architect

and build a crazy house,

or I could be a scientist

and grow a super mouse.

I'd like to be a soccer star
and score a million goals,

or I could drive a *digger truck
and dig enormous holes.

I want to be a *hairdresser

and cut the latest styles.

And then I'll be a *zookeeper

and feed the *crocodiles.

I'd like to be a farmer, too.

I think it would be nice.

I'll raise some chickens and some pigs,

and I can grow some rice.

I could be a businesswoman.
Now wouldn't **that** be funny?
I want to start a company,
and make a lot of money.

But then I'll give it all away,
to children who are poor.
I hope to make their lives become
much better than before.

Next I'll be the President.

I think that would be great.

I'll eat ice cream all day long,

and get up really late.

When I'm ninety-nine years old,

I'll retire in *San Francisco.

I'll play golf, go shopping and...

go dancing in the disco!

Who knows what the future *holds?

Who knows what I'll be?

So many different jobs to do.

We'll have to wait and see.

Jenny *wondered how she'd done.

She got a big surprise.

The *judges gave her perfect marks,

and said she'd won first prize!

生字表

（詞性以縮寫表示：*v.* 動詞，*n.* 名詞）

我的志願

p. 3

各位小姐和先生，請仔細洗耳恭聽。
演講比賽在今天，題目是我的志願：

p. 5

我長大後要教書，教遍大小各學府；
做起校長我最行，所有校規任我訂。

p. 6～7

想當馬戲團小丑，鋼索搖晃慢步走。
消防隊員也不錯，奮不顧身去救火。

p. 9

心臟科醫生也行，這樣才能救人命。
（白色制服很好看，手術刀也拿來玩。）

p. 10

電影明星我最愛，開著名車真光彩。
時裝皇后也不賴，高級雜誌露身材。

p. 13

太空人我也要做，星際飛行樂趣多，
在月球上蓋都市，家住火星真舒適。

p. 14～15

我的數學沒得比，銀行櫃員沒問題。
然後當兵真神氣，開著戰車了不起。

p. 16～17

還要當個大畫家，戴起怪帽來畫畫。
相撲選手實在酷，我願變成大胖豬。

p. 18～19

當建築師不意外，蓋棟房子很古怪。
科學家非常傑出，飼養超級大老鼠。

p. 20～21

足球明星我也行，射門得分數不清。
也想當怪手司機，挖個大洞不見底。

p. 22～23

我願做個美髮師，剪出新潮的樣式。
動物園我也要去，當管理員餵鱷魚。

p. 24～25

我也想要當農夫，那種生活真羨慕。
養雞之外又養豬，下田耕作種五穀。

p. 26

女企業家也很妙，那樣肯定很好笑，
開家公司當老闆，認真工作有錢賺。

p. 27

但是我會很慷慨，錢都捐給窮小孩，
讓他們生活改善，不愁吃也不愁穿。

p. 29

最後我要做總統，這樣一定很光榮，
整天都吃冰淇淋，睡到很晚才過癮。

p. 30

活到九十九歲時，退休住在三藩市，
逛街再打高爾夫，又去迪斯可跳舞。

p. 32

未來怎樣天曉得？誰能知道會如何？
好多行業可以做，看來得以後再說。

p. 33

演講完畢看分數，大吃一驚想歡呼，
裁判都給她好評，說她贏得第一名！

- 說說唱唱學韻文第 44 頁答案：

My math is good so I can be
a teller in a bank.
I will join the army next,
so I can drive a tank.

blank
sank
thank

Next I'll be an architect
and build a crazy house,
or I could be a scientist
and grow a super mouse.

blouse
louse
douse

I'd like to be a farmer, too.
I think it would be nice.
I'll raise some chickens and some pigs,
and I can grow some rice.

dice
mice
slice
nice

說說唱唱學韻文

珍妮的故事是由富有韻律感的韻文組成，而要判斷兩個英文字有沒有押韻，就是看這兩個字的結尾聽起來像不像；例如cat和hat就是押韻的字。接下來我們要介紹一個叫做「字彙家族」(word family) 的概念，可以做為學習英文押韻的基礎！

 請跟著CD的第四首，大聲的唸出以下的字：

bake　　take　　cake

有沒有發現這些字的結尾聽起來都很像呢？因為它們都是屬於 –ake 家族的字喔！

 再看看下面這一組字，跟著CD的第五首，將它們大聲的唸出來：

feet　　greet　　meet

發現了嗎？這是屬於 –eet 這個字彙家族的字！

請跟著CD的第六首一起大聲唸出下面的這首童詩。你能不能找出有哪幾個韻腳是屬於同樣的字彙家族呢？

Good Night, Sleep Tight

Good night,
sleep tight,
don't let the bedbugs bite.
Wake up bright
in the morning light,
to do what's right
with all your might.

Good night,
sleep tight,
don't let the bedbugs bite.
And if they do
then take your shoe,
and knock them till
they're black and blue!

你找出韻腳的字彙家族了嗎？

ight──night, tight, bright, light, right, might

有沒有發現，屬於同一個字彙家族的字一定都是押韻的，但押韻的字卻不一定屬於同一個字彙家族喔！像上面那首詩中，藍色的字也都是互相押韻的，卻不屬於同一個字彙家族！

請跟著CD的第七首一起唸，找出本頁三組句子韻腳的字彙家族，再聽CD第八首，從下面粉紅色框中，挑出相同字彙家族的字，寫在虛線框框裡。

blouse	dice	mice	slice	thank
blank	louse	sank	douse	nice

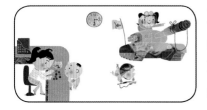

My math is good so I can be
a teller in a bank.
I will join the army next,
so I can drive a tank.

blank
sank
thank

Next I'll be an architect
and build a crazy house,
or I could be a scientist
and grow a super mouse.

I'd like to be a farmer, too.
I think it would be nice.
I'll raise some chickens and some pigs,
and I can grow some rice.

（答案請見第 41 頁）

請跟著CD的第九首一起大聲朗誦並唱出這首童謠「我在鐵道上工作」。最後還可以跟著伴奏自己獨唱一次！

I've Been Working on the Railroad

I've been working on the railroad,
all the livelong day.
I've been working on the railroad,
to pass the time away.
Don't you hear the whistle blowing?
Rise up so early in the morn.
Don't you hear the captain shouting
"Dinah, blow your horn"?
Dinah, won't you blow,
Dinah, won't you blow,
Dinah, won't you blow your horn, your horn?
Dinah, won't you blow,
Dinah, won't you blow,
Dinah, won't you blow your horn?

關於作者

Peter Wilds has authored and co-authored over a dozen books for young people. He has been living in Taiwan since 1993. He currently makes his home in Taichung with his wife and two sons.

Peter Wilds 為青少年寫了很多書，有自己獨立創作的、也有與人合著的。自 1993 年起他就住在台灣了，目前和妻子及兩個兒子住在台中。

關於繪者

蔡兆倫
專長以及興趣：漫畫 + 插畫 + 圖畫書

關於譯者

貪婪的毛毛蟲，終日啃食忙，爬在一葉葉的文字上，一心只想換上新衣裳。

只要填飽一肚子的好奇，趕快長出翅膀，橫著吃拼音字，還是直著吃方塊字，都不妨。

——王盟雄

47

童詩、童心與韻文

　　　　《敲敲節奏說韻文》系列包括三本童書，採用詩歌的形式，為小讀者敘說小女孩珍妮的故事。《我的志願》說的是珍妮的二十五個志願。《越幫越忙》說的是珍妮一片好心幫媽媽做家事。《媽咪，颱風是什麼？》說的是珍妮對颱風的想像。三個故事都以兒童的觀點、兒童的想法來寫，容易引起孩子的會心和共鳴，具有兒童文學的價值和趣味。

　　　　原作是英文，用淺顯流暢的文字寫童詩。句子都很短，容易學，容易記，背誦不費力。很重視押韻，所以唸起來很好聽。這些優點，使這三本書成為兒童學習英語的理想教材。

　　　　因為這是一套中英雙語童書，所以三本書都附有中文翻譯，作為呼應，一樣是短短的句子，一樣是重視押韻，既可以幫助兒童了解原

文的意思和趣味，又可以避免頻頻翻閱字典的繁瑣而削弱了學習的樂趣。 想為兒童選擇英語課外讀物的家長和老師， 這三本書值得一試。

　　　　　　　　　　　　兒童文學作家 林良

珍妮是個古靈精怪的小女孩，在「敲敲節奏說韻文」系列中，她以韻文的方式敘述生活中的趣事，有節奏感的故事聽起來好有趣；她教大家什麼是押韻，還帶小讀者一起唱童謠；她的世界如此豐富，你一定不能錯過！

Children's Verses Series
敲敲節奏說韻文系列

Peter Wilds／著　蔡兆倫／繪　王盟雄／譯
精裝／附中英雙語朗讀CD／全套三本
具基礎英文閱讀能力者（國小4～6年級）適讀

1 What Is a Typhoon, Mommy?　媽咪，颱風是什麼？

2 What I Want to Be　我的志願

3 Jenny Helps Do the Housework　越幫越忙

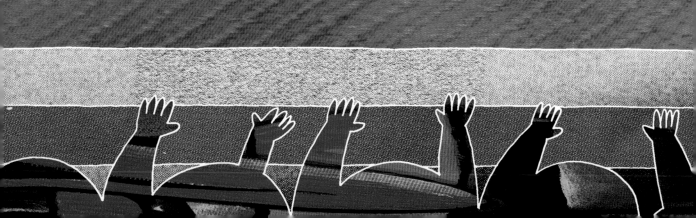

BUG BUDDIES SERIES 我的昆蟲朋友系列

具基礎英文閱讀能力者（國小4～6年級）適讀

文•Kriss Erickson　　圖•卡圖工作室

我有幾個昆蟲好朋友，各個都有自己奇怪的特性，讓他們有點煩惱；可是這樣的不同，卻帶給他們意想不到的驚奇與結果！

「我的昆蟲朋友」共有五個：

1. Bumpy's Crazy Tail　　邦皮的瘋狂尾巴
2. Fleet's Sticky Feet　　飛麗的黏腳丫
3. Stilt's Stick Problem　　史提的大麻煩
4. Macy's Strange Snacks　　莓西的怪點心
5. Stinky's Funny Scent　　丁奇的怪味道

—附中英雙語CD—

國家圖書館出版品預行編目資料

What I Want to Be:我的志願 / Peter Wilds著;蔡兆倫
繪;王盟雄譯.－－初版二刷.－－臺北市:三民, 2015
面; 公分.－－(Fun心讀雙語叢書.敲敲節奏說
韻文系列)
ISBN 978-957-14-4678-3 (精裝)
1.英國語言－讀本

523.38   95025212

© **What I Want to Be**
—— 我的志願

著 作 人	Peter Wilds
繪 者	蔡兆倫
譯 者	王盟雄
發 行 人	劉振強
著作財產權人	三民書局股份有限公司
發 行 所	三民書局股份有限公司
	地址 臺北市復興北路386號
	電話 (02)25006600
	郵撥帳號 0009998-5
門 市 部	(復北店)臺北市復興北路386號
	(重南店)臺北市重慶南路一段61號
出版日期	初版一刷 2007年1月
	初版二刷 2015年1月
編 號	S 806941

行政院新聞局登記證局版臺業字第〇二〇〇號

有著作權·不准侵害

ISBN 978-957-14-4678-3 (精裝)

http://www.sanmin.com.tw 三民網路書店